# The Sanders Corner Book of Poems

## By John Allwork

With my best Wishes

John P. Allwork.

www.thegardeningpoet.co.uk.

The Sanders Corner Book of Poems
By John Allwork


Published by Allwork in Rhyme Publications

ISBN 978-0-9570754-0-5


Printed by:
Images
72 Chase Side
Enfield
Middlesex
EN2 6NX

www.images-pdc.co.uk

To Dad.

Frederick Arthur George
Allwork.

The R.A.F. Carpenter
Who built our lives.
Now at peace beneath
His Enfield skies.

# Poems from a Gardener

## A little bit of Ye Olde England

# About This Book
## From Sanders Corner, Crews Hill, Enfield.

A Corner Book – a book to be placed in the reading corners of a home, to be read and rested, then read again. Many of the poems were written whilst I was working at Sanders Corner. Hence the name "The Sanders Corner Book of Poems."

The poems have been written over a period of forty years, as I worked in various horticultural and viticultural establishments in England and France – always making poetry notes as I worked. But it was at Crews Hill where I wrote most of the poems and redeveloped previously written works into their present form.

The Crews Hill area has seen a great change – as mentioned in some of my poems – The Old Plough Pub at Sanders Corner which housed the offices of the London Aquatic

Nursery, now gone. This building which gave its name to the corner has been demolished, (all that remains is the memory of a name) and the Nursery land around it flattened.

I worked for twenty two years as a plant propagator for the London Aquatic Company, and this book is a little tribute to the people I've met, who worked in this changing Crews Hill area, best years of my life!

Another place that's changing and mentioned in my poems is Exeter, its quayside and canal – the canal being the oldest in England, and brought riches to the City of Exeter. The canal allows safe boat passage from the sea to the Exeter Basin where boats can be lifted out on to the massive granite quayside where they can be repaired and maintained. This facility of being able to work on the boats is now under threat by an encroaching housing development – which will change the historic use of this area, hence a few poems about Exeter, and the beautiful surrounding landscape of Devon.

Other poems are about different places I've visited around England and even France – and many general observations on life. Religion and politics are skimmed over – in fact, as a gardener the only Political Party I'd vote for, is the Party who would put forward the proposal to raise the soil level by three feet, to save me having to bend down so far when I'm weeding!
Towards the end of the book is a section for children; among these poems are some fictional characters which I hope will raise a few smiles.
The subject matter of the poems vary greatly, but at its heart, the Sanders Corner Book of Poems, is a book that takes a look at life!

# Acknowledgements

Many thanks to my wife Myra and my daughters Emma and Jenny for listening to many recitals of my poems and even encouraging me to get them into a book form at last!
Thanks to Emma and Jenny for hours of typing and for Jenny doing the art work on the front cover and other illustrations. And here I'd like to thank Lucy Satchell for her photo of the Sand dunes, James Homer for his picture of leaves, and Mrs Alison Green for allowing me to take photos of her garden included in this book.

I also thank my sister Sally Cousins for typing out some early copies of my poems and for providing, with her husband Terry, inspirational barbeque meals at their home in Puckeridge.
Now to my brother Bill Allwork and his boat the "CHARLES DIBDIN" in Exeter, Devon. A great big thank you for the superb sunny holidays onboard the boat on the river Exe, and off to Dartmouth and France. The surrounding West Country scenery certainly inspired the Devon poems, Exeter and Topsham being special towns to visit. Thanks brother, thanks for your time and effort.

A final thanks to my mother May Allwork who encouraged me from an early age to take an interest in the words which make up poems and stories. Also for those early walks in our local parks and woods; Forty Hill, Whitewebbs etc. Well done mum and dad for being there!

And, a big thank you to my gardening customers!

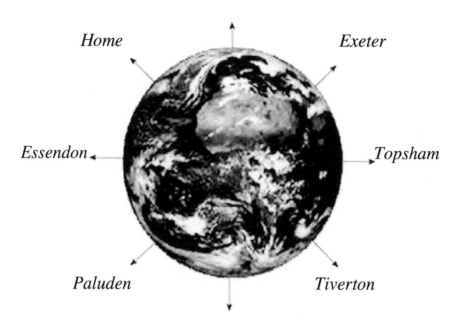

*Enfield*

*Home*

*Exeter*

*Essendon*

*Topsham*

*Paluden*

*Tiverton*

*Mickleton*

# Some of my Poem Places.

To be said as quickly as possible,

Enfield, Exeter,
Topsham, Tiverton,
Mickleton, Paluden,
Essendon, Home!

# Contents

A lovely reason

The Sun came out this morning
And kissed me on the head.
I thought . . .
Now THERE'S a lovely reason,
For getting out of BED!


J.J.J.      John Allwork

# IN ENGLAND BEATS A HEART

I love our fields of football,
And our county cricket games.
I follow the flowing rugby,
And those famous sporting names.

I watch the London Marathon,
And the Boat Race from the start,
And I wish to say, I love our ways
For in England beats a heart!

I love our island coastline . . .
Its giant cliffs and gentle bays.
Its sailing boats and barges
And, our inland waterways.

I watch our country springtime,
And our trees, they play their part,
In the blossoming of a landscape
For, in England beats a heart!

I love our island people
Different accents, and comic flair.
One thing we have in common
Is this land that we all share!

I watch our tradesmen selling
From a stall or market cart,
And THERE you'd see tradition
For, in England beats a heart!

I love our English Gardens,
And our annual village shows.
Where the produce of the gardens,
Are proudly placed in rows.

And where I watch England's Judges
Judge the winning treacle tart.
You could only be in England
For, in England beats a heart.

I love our Fireworks Night,
Skies flash as if aflame!
Our rockets race with history . . .
And, Guy Fawkes' the man we blame!

I watch our Christmas shoppers,
Buying gifts and Christmas Art,
To make our homes, more homely
For, in England beats a heart!

I love our English tea shop
With, "Tea and cakes for two!"
And the Pub in the village
With, a pint of home made brew.

I treasure our tradition . . .
As you've gathered from the start.
And I wish to say, I love our ways
For, in England beats my heart!


J.J.J.   John Allwork.

# The Wedding That Held the World

The Buckingham Balcony held the Bucklebury Bride,
Her husband, Prince William held Her by his side!
The Nation held this couple close to its heart.
The World watched their wedding, this LIVE work of ART!

Uniforms, helmets, medals and swords,
A wedding with the famous, Queens, Princes and Lords!
Televisions, cameras, reporters and cables,
Sniffer dogs, soldiers, and horses from stables!

In Westminster Abbey, a lush line of green trees,
A symbol of the Country, to set Catherine at ease.
Her white wedding dress with delicate lace,
A romantic reminder of a young Princess Grace.

But one memory of Catherine will last quite a while...
Her steady walk through the Abbey, and her wonderful smile.
Behind Catherine came Pippa – just perfection in poise,
Such a sight of delight for – YES, all of the boys!

Wedding vows said with slight nerves of the face,
But all lines well spoken, not a word out of place.
Then up to the Balcony for a show stopping scene,
Along with Princes, a Duke, and Elizabeth our Queen!

Two youngsters, two kisses, held TWO BILLION people!
Of past happy events we've not seen an equal.
From Kate of the Country, to PRINCESS in a day!
You could HEAR London cheering every step of the way!

In a party performance that couldn't be pipped...
A clergyman who cartwheeled and a policeman who tripped!
On a day that brought Britain back to being GREAT!
Well done to William, and our Royal country Kate!


J.J.J.    John Allwork

'Bordering on Perfection' Theobalds Farm
House Garden.

# The Nursery Road

The Nursery Road to Crews Hill Station,
Fed the growers, who fed a nation,
With 'toms and 'cues from a greenhouse maze
Those salad crops, of those salad days.

Now a weekend cavalcade of cars
Cruises to the Crews Hill bars.
The Plough, a pub with rural name,
But a rural rejoice of rustic fame.

The plough that once broke stubborn soil
Where stubborn men no longer toil.
Both plough and man a common fate :-
A redundant tool, and its redundant mate.

On the road now speeds " turbo'' commuter,
Both country dweller and country polluter.
His home with cars that show his class,
On land once covered by bright clean glass.

Those greenhouses with glass to spare,
Removed, or rotted, and land laid bare.
Where flowers flourished near a meadow track,
Now coldly covered by hard tarmac.

The pressure is on for the nursery space
And the growing need of a parking place.
Those greenhouses with growing crops,
Converted to halls of static shops.

The Nursery Road to Crews Hill Station,
Supplies the " growers'' who supply a nation.
This modern marketing, itself no sin,
But plants once grown, are now brought in !


J.J.J.    John Allwork

# TAPLOW

The land of the rising bum


We love to toil at Taplow,
Where strangers rarely stray,
And where a moon comes out mischievously,
In the middle of the day.

Much of the glass is missing
In this greenhouse of old wood,
This vents the passing air,
As only such a structure could.

It was on this greenhouse land,
With its workers fresh and new,
We saw that part of a person,
Normally spared from view.

A lad so stressed with work,
Expressed an inner feeling,
He raised his rear in the air
At a temporary greenhouse ceiling.

And in dropping down his pants,
He revealed a mischievous moon
Towering over his trousers
In the early afternoon.

The Boss saw this sphere,
And had nightmares for a week,
He'd wanted to kick the rear
And not tolerate the cheek.

But, with ageing one gets cautious
And his courage began to melt . . .
Now he's haunted by that sight
Of what lies below a belt!

The greenhouse has now fallen,
Beneath it lies the proof,
Of the land where we laboured
In our horticultural youth.

Maybe in retirement we'll think
Of that, "Taplow Time" . . . .
And the memory of the moment
When a "Moon" was seen to shine!

Oh! We'd love to toil at Taplow,
Where strangers rarely stray,
And where a moon came out mischievously
In the middle of the day!

J.J.J.    John Allwork

# Wages
## And
## THE COMPANY POLICY

I'd liked to have given you more me boys,
I'd liked to have given you more.
But we're a Firm still trading,
Unlike the Firm next door!

My holiday's booked a year in advance,
You take yours when you get the chance.
I could change my car this year if I like,
But if I were you I'd stick with your bike!

I'd liked to have given you more me boys,
I'd liked to have given you more!

My dinners out, and lunch in the Pub,
Takes the place of more envious grub
The staff with their sandwiches of bread and cheeses,
Now THAT'S the food that really pleases!

I'd liked to have joined you for lunch me boys,
I'd liked to have joined you for lunch!

The weather's bad, a day of rain,
Work winds on just the same!
The staff with their clothes all wet and mucky
But, with waterproof trousers BOY, you aren't half lucky!

I'd liked to have worked in the rain me boys,
I'd liked to have worked in the rain!

Orders go out, we work round the clock,
Despatching the plants, we've no time to stop.
A customer arrives, "My order's ready!" he sighs,
And receives his goods, with tears in his eyes!

Saying:
"I'd liked to have bought you a drink me boys,
I'd liked to have bought you a drink!"

The Festive Time comes once again,
To some of us it's such a pain.
The same Christmas bonus once more this year,
But, what's that phrase we expect to hear . . .

I'D LIKED TO HAVE GIVEN YOU MORE ME BOYS,
I'D LIKED TO HAVE GIVEN YOU MORE.
BUT WE'RE A FIRM STILL TRADING,
UNLIKE THE FIRM NEXT DOOR !


J.J.J.    John Allwork

# A DREAM
## The last Bonussaurus

I mumbled, "A bonus saw us fed last year."
"A bonus saw us spread some cheer . . . ."
My sleepy words just weren't that clear,
Wife said, " Isn't a Bonussaurus dead my Dear ?"

Z Z Z Z

I dozed off dreaming, in a comfy chair,
Of a land where Pigs fly through the air!
Where big Bonussaurus play as they please,
And Pay Packets frequently grow on trees!

Now, these Bonussaurus used to roam,
Just twice a year and then go home.
They'd come to our work place on Week 19
And frolic in our financial scene.

They grazed on profits grown in a year,
The bigger the profits the bigger their rear.
For Fat Cats, they helped swell their prides,
For weaker creatures, they would offer rides.

A smaller member of their Pack
Would appear at Christmas, then race back.
But this Bonussaurus spread some cheer,
In those final days of a parting year!

A Terry tactful, of the words to use,
Once enquired about, "Bonussaurus News"
He was simply told he had to wait . . .
And further enquiries may harm their fate!

Z Z Z Z

The Wife awoke me, much to my surprise
Patted my head and said, " Please don't rise !"
" I've looked that word up, in my Thesaurus . . ."
" I'm afraid there is no Bonussaurus !"


J.J.J.    John Allwork

# The Bubble Dibble Hat Man

His human frame hadn't a brain,
But seldom he'd miss that at all,
Except for the day, his words went astray,
As this poem I hope will recall.

No one was quicker, in warning of litter,
That blew around our front yard.
But the words Hat Man used, to announce this News
Impressed, Yours truly. . . " The Bard ."

So desperate to warn of the litter like storm,
And Hat Man tried, most exceedingly hard.
But try as he might to mouth the words right,
He found his tongue caught completely off guard !

With an excited shout, letters jumbled about,
His lack of brain couldn't rectify that !
So his words of despair :- "There's rubbish everywhere!"
Changed to :- "Bubble, Dibble and Hat!"

You could tell by our eyes the instant surprise,
As these words Hat Man tried to explain . . .
Are words you can say, when your brain's gone astray
And can be repeated again and again.

So, when lost for a phrase, in a literary haze,
And your conversation has fallen quite flat.
Remember to use , three words from this Muse . . .
Our friends :- BUBBLE, DIBBLE and HAT !

Bubble dibble hat, bubble dibble hat.
Bounces to the beat of a train on a track.
Bubble dibble hat, bubble dibble hat,
An expression unique?  Well, most certainly THAT !

J.J.J.    John Allwork

THE PLAY . . .          THE AUTUMN WAGE REVIEW
                        A seasonal problem.

THE ACTORS . . .        SERF and MASTER
                        And special guest.

THE SETTING . . .       Serf seated in silent thought,
             Master on a plinth, smoking more than he ought.


                ·····································
             THE AUTUMN WAGE REVIEW
Early Spring.

Master      "With my staff expecting an annual rise,
                I thought an Autumn wage review was wise;
                For this keeps them guessing throughout the year,
                Of when the Autumn is actually here!"
Months later.

  Serf         The Autumn review, not to be underrated,
                For Master seems pensive, and agitated.
                This Autumn's arrival is still not clear,
                Just when is Autumn coming this year?

  Master      "Autumn follows Summer, as a general rule,
                But this year's Summer was rather cool;
                So we leapt from Spring, in one fell swoop,
                And landed in Winter – what a scoop!"

  Master      "So no need to review the Autumn rise,
                You've missed it this year..."

  Serf            Surprise, Surprise!

                              30

| Master | "But come next Spring I will promise anew<br>And think once again about an Autumn review." |
|---|---|
| Serf | "HUMPH!" |
| Master | Trying to change the subject;<br><br>"Now there are three promises that men break<br>the most:-<br>One; Your cheque's been written, it's in the post.<br>Two; I love only you, my darling, my dear!..." |
| Serf | "And THREE, I'll review the wages in the<br>Autumn this year!" |
| Master | "The recession you know has caused quite a slump,<br>And our profits have fallen, they made quite a bump.<br>Giving staff more money, is one of life's joys..." |
| Serf | "Yerr, but we've heard this before, haven't we boys!" |
| Master | "HUMPH!" |
| Serf | "We'd look forward to Christmas, but for the myth-<br>That this year it's changed from the Twenty-Fifth!<br>For if Autumn's abandoned, then who can tell,<br>He may even cancel the day of Noel!" |

Enter Scrooge,
Special guest.

"Now this setting IS familiar, the sentiment, I know,
But your scenery is drab – you need more snow!
And the lighting was by gas, it gave a warmer glow…
But, it's still the same old firm I knew- a hundred years ago!"

THE CLOSE OF PLAY…

Serf tries to imagine the firm's fiscal dream,
Master disappears from sight, his smoking has filled the scene!

J.J.J.    John Allwork

# The London Aquatic Company
## ( L.A.C. our old Nursery)

"Do you remember, that day when…?"
"Ah yes, we were so much younger then!"


The Nursery gates, no need to open,
No Nursery workers, no word spoken.
The morning post, no longer needed,
And empty seed trays, no longer seeded.
Our rushes tall and the slender reed,
Had all been sown from our saved seed.
This country corner of an Enfield road,
Was once a home to frog and toad.

No more the thirsty workers race
Into the crowded kitchen space.
Where tea and toast and world affairs
Were digested on old wooden chairs.
That game of Crib a lunchtime must,
Its board and cards now gather dust.
Both young and old were keen to play . . .
And,  time stood timeless in the day.

The tanks where coloured goldfish swam,
Where the Nursery's history first began,
Now dry and empty,  no fishy tails
To splash new life into springtime sales.
We produced new plants on this Nursery plot,
Different Iris types and,  Forget–me–not . . .
There's no game of Crib, no winning shout,
For our Nursery now has just,  pegged out . . .


J.J.J.   John Allwork

34

# Crews Hill Hedges.

Our hedges and "growing-nurseries"
Now up-rooted and in decline,
Once flourished from the "Fallow Buck"
To the "Plough" and railway line.

Although hidden little nurseries,
People knew just where to stop.
Now a bill-boarded selling point,
That doesn't grow a crop!

So very little home grown,
We're fed by foreign hordes.
Just one thing left that's home produced...
Our advertising boards!

We fly:- "Produce from Portugal"
"Fresh fruit from France," with ease.
What is the difficulty of fetching fruit
From British fruiting trees?

We now import flowers ,
From a continental store.
The very flowers Crews Hill grew,
And was so famous for!

The nursery, a seat of learning,
For an industry and career.
Now gone this green profession,
"They don't grow no plants HERE!"

This new imported flora,
Demands a clear nursery site.
Hence the removal of the hedges,
Completed almost overnight!

Those yards, and yards, of hedgerows,
Removed by nurseries as they grew.
For the HOME-GROWN-HEDGE had hidden,
The foreign flowers from view!

Our hedges and growing nurseries,
In prime production for a time.
Once flourished from the "Fallow Buck",
To the "Plough" and railway line!

J.J.J.    John Allwork

Sanders Corner

# Sanders Corner

## EN2 9DH Demolished History

At Sanders Corner stood the former
Plough Pub and nursery site.
Once a haven for aquatic plants,
Once a drinking man's delight!

Those boozy bars, and water lily stars,
Have been lifted from the land.
No longer a corner full of flowers,
Where a pub building stood so grand!

The Old Plough Pub had a Winkle club,
Taking men to a seaside shore.
There's a famous photo of Pub and Club,
Taken in Nineteen Thirty Four!

What thoughts would they have now,
If they could see this place?
Of their building, the Old Plough Pub,
There remains,  not a trace!

Was it modernizing man,
Who triggered the building's fall?
Or some accidental event?
I'm sure, someone knows it all!

No old Pub, nor nursery plants,
Behind new boundary fence confines.
Just a flattened weedy wasteland,
Sees man, "moving with the times!"


J.J.J.    John Allwork

To a friend, who fell head first,
off a sports stadium balcony, whilst doing a handstand
-and is now full recovered.


# A.H.H.

## Adam Handstand Haverill.

Handstand Haverill showed off his skill,
Handstand Haverill fell off the sill.
All the sports stadium all gathered around,
To see his legs in the air and his head in the ground.

What was he doing – well might one wonder,
Re-visiting friends – those from down under?
He'd been to New Zealand a land full of mirth,
And tried to go back there straight through the Earth!

To fly by Quantas is the usual route,
Not for our Adam who was saving his loot.
He thought his head was as hard as a conker,
Realized too late, A.H.H. what a plonker!

So keep head in the air where it's best seen,
And enjoy your birthday, when you're eighteen.
We join together in a requestful refrain,
Please dear Adam don't do it again!


J.J.J.    John Allwork

'Forty Hall'

# In defence of Forty Hall

Through gate and garden, fence and field,
Across lake and lawn, a house revealed.
That square of house, with chimneys tall,
It's Raynton's home, our Forty Hall !

The gaggle of geese that grazed the grass,
And pursued the public as they passed,
Forty's feathered farmyard fowl,
Its guardians then, we're its guardians now !

Parks and gardens may come and go,
Some old Enfield trees have gone,( we know ).
While at Forty Hall a path leads through
To a gardener's garden, where His tree grew !

Give a passing thought to that effort made,
By the man in the garden, with sapling and spade.
He planted a Cedar for us to enjoy,
Now a symbol of many we've come to destroy!

His Cedar spread forming noble tiers,
Enfield's history for hundreds of years.
Those fan like branches needled and coned,
In this private garden, now public owned.

Our Parks and trees are safe indeed,
While they fulfill a certain need.
How safe and sound our Greenbelt land,
Would a builder HERE dare lay a hand ?

At Forty Hall, once Raynton's Home,
Those chimneys tall, see the public roam.
BUT, if destructive planners plan Forty's fate,
Would its sole defence be its garden gate ?


J.J.J.    John Allwork

# The M25

A Farmyard fresh with flowers and fruit,
An old tree stump, its forgotten root.
The sunken hollow of a hidden pond...
Flattened by Law and the Government's wand!

Develop, develop this chosen land,
A ring road's needed to make life grand.
A greater stretch of metaled road,
To carry more cars with a greater load.

The field had been empty, but for some trees.
On still days, silence – not even a breeze.
There on high sung the skylark of peace,
Now down below shrieks the highway police!

They scream to an accident, with blue flashing light,
And come to the carnage, this motorway blight.
A highway through land where men used to dwell,
Where Motorway Man said "All would be well."

It encircles the City, it encircles the towns,
It crosses the valleys, it crosses the Downs.
And sucks out oxygen, and stifles the air,
Increasing asthma and our medical care.

It tramples on toads and flattens the frogs,
This team of traffic competes with the Gods ...
But, Humans now share with worty old toads –
A pathway to Heaven, via mighty new roads!

J.J.J.    John Allwork

# The Millennium Vote
For the year 2000

Though empty-headed Enfield man,
Built on sites where The Town began.
There still stands a medieval face,
That solitary square of the Market Place.

And the Church which chimes an hourly prayer,
To timeless traders on this stoney square.
Perhaps just history they are themselves,
Where Old England trades, and Enfield dwells.

For around The Town with links of might,
A Supermarket chain pulls tight.
Squeezing out the old shopping place,
As smaller shops fall out of grace.

The Savoy Cinema, will solemnly close,
Like in a Western sunset, it gradually goes.
Its site is needed for the purposeful gain,
Of one more link in a Supermarket chain!

They'll start perhaps The Town anew,
A trading place, with no Church view!
So Enfield planners please take note,
Before deciding, the Millennium vote.

Keep alive the historic heart of Town,
Within steepled spires of Enfield's Crown.
For throughout the country history fades,
As Millennium Man now fast upgrades!

For in England's fields and cities stand,
Our history green, and our history grand.
However, it's lost LOCAL history I most bemoan...
England's my country, but Enfield's my home!


J.J.J.   John Allwork

## Planet Pesco

The spreading plague of Pesco Stores,
Will soon be seen from all front doors.
Rising up from road to road,
Across the Channel then around the Globe.

Stores built quicker than town houses,
With a flood of light for foods and trousers.
Enticing the shopper to be a greedy gannet,
Their stores of light, beam from our Planet.

A star like pattern to be seen from space,
The constellation of Pesco, on our Planet's face.
Their lights will twinkle, and look quite pretty,
As they consume the World, "Now that's a pity."

But never mind – there's a new Pesco plan,
A giant shopping leap for modern man.
Expansion's due, they need more space
And they think the Moon is just the place!

Shoppers will gather in a departure lounge,
They'll be full of hope and, Moon Pesco bound.
A new shopping line with flags unfurled,
As Planet Pesco starts a new, BRAND WORLD.


J.J.J.   John Allwork

# Winter Shopping

Through drizzle rain to dazzle haven,
Winter shopping on a watery night.
Shopping malls, moisture laden,
Bathing liquid assets in liquid light.

The sodden storm of shopping hordes,
Hoping to save , by spending money.
Programmed, by special-offer boards,
Those tempting treats, so bright and sunny.

The empty trolleys fill with food –
Steel wire stomachs with a wobbly wheel.
Dateless music , for a brain-dead mood,
Numbs the mind so the adverts appeal.

Greeting friends , in a food hall frenzy,
The shopping  Palace becomes a home.
Arrange to see the friends next  Wednesday,
Now where's that child who began to roam ?

The endless line of cashiers waiting,
To process products picked in the store.
Rain outside , falls unabating ---
Cosy inside , so we'll purchase more!

The cash-desk consumes its gullet of goods,
Bar-coded messages race to the till.
Back to the rain, so up with the hoods,
Shopping weighs heavy – and so does the BILL !


J.J.J.    John Allwork

# A plea for the A and E

Give praise to be, to the A and E,
A service our citizens share.
I question those, wishing to close,
Chase Farm and OUR medical care!

The land would be sold, for fortunes in gold,
With new people quickly housed there.
But where will THEY go when they grow old,
And in need of some hospital care?

Whether you're old, whether you're young,
Or whether you're still, yet to be!
A service required and SO much desired,
Is that of a LIVE A and E.

J.J.J.    John Allwork

50

Lumpy and Grumpy

If you awake  and

Just

At your work load ahead.

For, as time passes by,

Within a wink of an eye,

You'll soon be tucked up

Back in BED!

J.J.J.    John Allwork

# The Best of Beer.

Always drink the best of Beer,
A Beer you really trust!
For I've heard that water is in some Beer,
If so…I'm doomed to RUST!


J.J.J.     John Allwork

# Mr Boozey's
# New year's resolution.

I swayed into the bathroom,
Familiar with my plight.
And held onto the wash basin
For my head was still in flight.

I gazed at a ghostly figure,
Mirrored over the bathroom shelf.
I wasn't frightened really
Because it was the image of myself.

I stared into the mirror,
I could not focus right.
It must have been that extra drink
I drank the other night.

I splashed water on my face,
And tried to comb my hair.
There was a vagueness about this person
Who did nothing else but stare.

So, I made myself a promise...
Drinks at parties were taboo!
But, I'd made this promise last year,
AND at last night's party, TOO!

J.J.J.   John Allwork

## Cruising round the carpet

I'm cruising round the carpet,
On a Sunday afternoon.
I seem to smile to myself,
And hum a football tune.

I've left my colleagues in the Pub,
And came home to greet the Misses,
But she's gone round to friends,
And left a pile of dirty dishes.

My dinner's in the dog,
And my dish is in the sink.
I'm in the dog house,
And I've had too much to drink.

I enjoyed the T.V. football,
In the Pub this afternoon.
But didn't realise the time,
Had come and gone so soon!

It's back to work on Monday,
And the mundane work routine.
I'm looking forward to next weekend,
To follow my favourite football team.

I'm now on my best behaviour, but . . .
The weekend can't come too soon!
When I'll be,
Cruising round the carpet
On the Sunday afternoon!


J.J.J.    John Allwork

# John's green bit of glory


This tiny piece of treasured turf
Removed from Hallowed Highbury earth,
Has now settled into Winchmore Hill
A memory green of past football skill.


No cheering crowd for this silent sod,
Upon whose face the famous trod.
From Highbury's stadium of brick and iron
To the humble garden of John O'Brien !


J.J.J.      John Allwork

# The White Lie

Ever found dull weather left you feeling blue,
Ever watched television, because there's nothing else to do.

"I haven't"

Ever stepped from a car, straight into a puddle.
Ever gone over drawn to get you out of trouble.

"I haven't"

Ever had the feeling you've been here before.
Ever wished a cheque was coming through your door.

"I haven't"

Ever been shopping and thought the bill, too high.
Ever been in a traffic jam, and wished that you could fly !

"I haven't"

Ever had a barbeque, where the weather turned to rain,
Ever remembered the sunny forecast and thought
THEY'VE GOT IT WRONG AGAIN!

"I haven't"

Ever thought your trousers, were getting rather tight.
Ever wanted the bathroom in the middle of the night.

"I haven't"

Ever had a nightmare, in which you couldn't hide.
Ever wished your mother was standing by your side.

"I haven't"

Ever answered a question, then found you've made a goof.
Ever told a white lie, just to hide the truth.

"I haven't...OOPS!"


J.J.J.    John Allwork

# Bus Stop Statues

Bus stop statues,
Still, not straight.
By the Bus sign,
They wait and wait.
This daily drudge,
Locked into time.
They pass through life,
In a single line.


J.J.J.     John Allwork

# A Lane in August
## Hertfordshire

## To Madge

This long beckoning finger
Wiggles round fields to form a frame,
Then dives beneath a wooded copse,
Now that's the country lane!

Such as we found in Hertfordshire,
On that hot, "Magical" day.
The barley was cut barley
While the whispering wheat held sway.

By Queen Hoo Hall we halted,
And walked beside it down a track.
To witness waves of ripened wheat,
This memory still ripples back.

Then on to Lordship Gardens
With its flowers, its views, its heat.
There we rested by the Lakeside
On a secluded, shaded, seat.

We motored on and upwards
And chugged up a little hill.
Just us, and the car were moving,
While the hot countryside lay still.

One minute in open sunshine,
The next, closed in by shade.
Then a moments view, through a fence or two,
There's a distant scene displayed.

That's the fun of a lane,
Views only last so long…
No sooner seen – that visionary dream,
And the treasured scene is gone.

We left behind those homely hills,
Bathed in summer's sunny beams.
Such warmth to remember when winter chills,
That "Magical" day of scenes!

J.J.J.    John Allwork

# The Advance of Winter.

The wind of Autumn sighs in pain,
As the howling Winter returns to maim:
Dimming our homes with a darkened sky
From a strangled sun long shadows fly.

The golden drifts of homeless leaves,
Plucked from twigs, by timeless thieves.
Placed in patterns in their store,
The coloured ground of the forest floor.

Stripped and stark, sway the limbs of trees,
Their pulse of life, now barely breathes.
While branches claw the air so cold,
Winter secures its chilling hold.

Cheerful colours from a Summer's hue
Now frosted, with an evening dew.
Those fragrant flowers once warm and bright,
Now scentless statues frozen white.

Restless ripples of imprisoned pools
Freeze glass hard as Autumn cools.
And windswept waters of a lapping lake
Stiffen to silence in Winters' wake.

The buzz of insects on the wing,
But a silent symphony until the Spring.
Flora and fauna in sleep so sound,
In their dormant dormitories under–ground.

The wind still breathes its mouthless air,
Arranging leaves with countless care,
To form the covers of a bed,
For all things living, and all things dead.


J.J.J.   John Allwork

# In a little corner of England

There is a corner of an English field
I see from an Essendon garden.
Where daily deer roam, to rabbits it's home
And the fox, its presence we pardon.

There's a slope to this field, this triangular shield
Of grass growing up to its edges.
Where tall bushes grow, in spring a flower show
This boundary of brambles in hedges.

The field slopes out of sight, to a dell of delight . . .
A low corner cushioned by trees.
Where peace you embrace, at nature's own pace
And time is spent well at ease.

On a cold winters' night, with curtains drawn tight
And I'm relaxed in a comfortable chair,
I think of this field, where the sun once revealed
The creatures that sunned themselves there.

Where deer daily roam, to rabbits it's home
And the fox, its presence we pardon.
In this little corner of an English field,
As seen from an Essendon garden !

J.J.J.    John Allwork

# A Sunday in Sussex

Sunday, descends into Sussex
Softly, as if winter's snow,
And relaxes the hearts of its people
Sleeping on in a bed-warming glow.

Sunday, may be heard in Sussex,
As it stirs to a tranquil tune.
The country calm of the morning
Feeds the YAWN of the afternoon.

Old lanes, linking village to village,
And streets, linked by Twittens in Towns;
Lie as quiet as the land they were built on,
Making UP to the peace of the Downs.

No cars, no carbon combustion,
No timetable tension today.
No need to rush to the station,
Before the 7.05 speeds away.

City suits, for work in the office,
Status clothes, a structured attire,
Symbolically removed on a Sunday,
At last , for one day, THEY retire.

Even, Lord Samuel Corruthers,
Becomes just plain, Sunday Sam.
As church bells in the village remind us –
In God's eyes we're seen as, just man !

Today, Bill the carpenter's  quiet,
He's finished Sir Stanley's new chair;
Men united as craftsman and client,
On this Sunday they peacefully share.

SO, what ever your week's occupation,
Your own title, or status or skill.
A Sunday in Sussex unites you,
Be you a Lord, or a Sir, or a BILL  !

J.J.J.    John Allwork

# To Ellen MacArthur

Ellen raced for a sea record,
And fought her way to fame.
She set out as sea lady
And sailed home as a Dame !


Ellen is home in England,
Safe from waves, whales and sharks.
She made our maritime history
As she sailed into our hearts !


Well done Ellen !


J.J.J.     John Allwork

# Jonny Wilkinson's
# Drop goal 2003

All England cheered together,
From Truro to Teesside Towns.
Across the valleys of Cumbria,
To Sussex and the Downs!

Good old Jonny!


J.J.J.        John Allwork

Emma and Jenny.

## Two Little School Girls,
## Emma and Jenny.

"I am Emma, I go to school,
And it doesn't cost me a penny."

"I will go to school as well this year,
I'm Emma's sister Jenny!"

"We will play our games
And learn friend's names,
And do our best to please."

"But, when we're in the playground
We'll try not to graze our knees!"

J.J.J.          John Allwork

# Bouncing Wishes

We stood, bouncing our wishes

Into the waves.

For every wish that bounced

There's one dream saved.

We stood, skimming stones

Into the sea.

Oh, why couldn't everyday

Be that carefree !

J.J.J.    John Allwork

'Sand Dunes' By Lucy Satchell.

*Summer*
*Waves of thought.*


*Cushioned in my hollow*
*I dozed upon the sands,*
*Letting grains of Time*
*Slip slowly through my hands.*


*Time itself has a stillness*
*As it's warmed by the Sun.*
*The very hour holds its breath*
*Between, the noonday and one.*


*The Sun was my blanket,*
*The Sand was my bed.*
*I could hear children playing*
*But, not a word they said.*

*Just the HUSH of foam*
*As it broke upon the beach.*
*I listened to the seaside,*
*As I slumbered in its heat.*


*There was no time in an hour,*
*Nor presence in a place.*
*No purpose in my lying here*
*Save, to fill a sunny space.*


*The sea shifted slightly,*
*Wet sand slowly dried.*
*Summer thoughts dissolved in rhythm*
*To the movement of the tide.*


*J.J.J.    John Allwork*

# My Childhood Bedroom

## Revisited

The hollow sound of an empty room,

Those dreams that came, then went too soon.

That echo of a childhood thought,

Then freely lost, now fondly sought!


The room in which I played for hours,

My toys all THEN, had magic powers.

Those toys now gone to playmates new,

And with them the child I outgrew!


J.J.J.   John Allwork

# The Spirit of Life

I'm as old as the hills and mountains,
I'm as young as a baby's first cry.
I leap with the water in fountains,
And I race with the clouds in the sky.

I'm as loud as a volcanic eruption,
I'm as quiet, as a passing thought.
I deal with death and destruction –
I help find the comfort that's sought.

I skip over valleys of water,
I skim over seas high and low.
I lift those hearts as they falter,
And restore a life that could go.

I cause a girl's heart to flutter,
When her boyfriend knocks at the door.
I cause the boyfriend to stutter,
When he asks to meet her once more.

I blossom in spring with the flowers,
And I shower with the evening rain.
I never count time by its hours,
The hours, make TIME , too mundane.

I'm harder than diamond and granite,
I'm softer, than a lover's first smile.
I've always been part of this Planet.
And believe me, THAT'S, quite a while !

I'm a front-line force for the living,
I'm there if you're stifled by strife.
Just reach for the power I am giving,
I'm in YOU, YOUR SPIRIT OF LIFE !

I'm as old as the hills and mountains,
I'm as young, as a baby's first cry.
And I leap through the water of fountains,
And I race through the clouds of the sky !


J.J.J.    John Allwork

# A Passing Thought

Every village has its graveyard,
Every town has graveyards wide.
Every city has its Cathedral,
Where only famous people died!

Every city has its workers,
Toiling beneath its Towers.
Are THEY buried in a Cathedral,
When they've run out of hours?

J.J.J.     John Allwork

# Johnny Jim Jam's Little Lane

I have this little lane I know
Where I wander to feel free,
And change through several characters
To return outwardly as *ME!*

My inner spirit is lifted,
My thoughts are free to fly.
My heart settles with whom it likes,
And I never question *WHY?*

…………..

I can pretend to be a sailor,
A rich man, poor man – thief.
Then return again, as me again…
Though, not always with relief.

I can dream I am a playboy,
Who leads a spicy life.
I can also be a Hermit,
Who's never troubled with a wife.

I can be a well known artist,
Who's preceded by his fame!
Instead of THIS individual,
Who's hardly known by name.

I can pretend I am on holiday –
A dreamer on the sands,
A head full of summer thoughts
And free from any plans.

I can be a bold explorer,
Who treks to far off places,
I'm known to people around the world,
And have friends from the rarest races.

BUT, it seems as I grow older
I return more often to this lane.
Asking many questions, that once
Never needed to explain.

What happened to past friends
With whom I was so fond?
Would some passing wave of memory
Now renew that friendly bond?

And would some recent written letter,
Perhaps now asking for a date.
Still find that friendly person
Though, it's many years too late?

...........

I have this little lane I know
Where I wander to feel free,
Where the characters of my lane
Are so much a part of *ME!*

Where my inner spirit is lifted
Where my thoughts are free to fly,
Where my heart settles with whom it likes
But now it's time to question *WHY?*

J.J.J.    John Allwork

# The Ignoramus

Derr    I'm an ignoramus,
      It's what my teacher said of ME.
      For when he asked ten questions,
      I'd only get two or three.

Hhhm    I tried hard with mafmatics,
      And I really battled with me sums.
      But I fought that 'trigernometry'
      'Ad sominck to do with guns.

Errr    Teacher stands me in the corner,
      Then writes a letter to me mum.
      The standing gives me exercise,
      'Cos it gets me off me bum.

Oh    I used to like Biology,
      But our teacher only lasted a week.
      He was taken off for Psychology
      They said he needed a sleep !

Ah    We started with reproduction,
      The subject to us was quite new.
      An Amoeba was used for introduction,
      BUT, do we really have to split into TWO !

Ehh    We did a bit of Shakespeare,
       We did, " The Taming of the Shrew"
       Though what happened to this rascal rodent
       I never really knew !

    Yerr    There are some blokes intelligent,
          Who fink that I'm a fool.
          But their carpentry's like that by an Elephant,
          They can't use their hands at all !

      Well    I won't go to University,
           I'm told I WON'T pass my exams.
           So I may become a Gardener,
           And get use to messing up me hands.

       ( Sigh )    But .... I may be better off than many
               By working along with the Mole.
               For, compared to gardeners
               There's more graduates on the dole !


             J.J.J.     John Allwork

Having to learn long Latin plant names and the relief
To come upon a simple name such as the one for the Daisy.
(Bellis perennis)

## Thanks for the Daisy

There's Matricaria matricarioides

Myriophyllum proserpinacoides

Metasequoia glyptostroboides

Polystichum acrostichioides

Lysimachia clethroides

Catalpa bignonioides

Ceratostigma plumbaginoides

Remembering these names,

Can drive you quite crazy!

Then there's, Bellis perennis,

Ah, thanks for the Daisy!

J.J.J.    John Allwork

'Leaf Photo' By James Homer

# An Autumn farewell to a Gardener

The lifeless leaf upon the land,
A garden missing its gardening hand.
Leaves fall to form a carpet grand,
In his favourite place, where he used to stand.

Garden tools wait where they belong,
The wheelbarrow waits to be lifted along.
Song birds silent, there's an energy gone,
This conductorless choir, in the midst of a song!

He'd stand in the greenhouse in his usual stance,
And gave new seeds a growing chance.
His spirit lives on with his personal plants,
Which still he surveys with a guardian's glance.

There's pots and gloves, seed trays and boots,
Old summer hats, and all weather suits,
Such a heavenly home for spiders and newts,
Among lifted plants, now drying their roots.

Those leaves that fell on his farewell day,
Drifted with words we whispered away,
And framed the thought, he'd wish to say . . .
"God bless my garden, where to work was to play!"

In memory of Malcolm

J.J.J.    John Allwork

84

'Fountain and Tulips' Theobalds Farm House garden.

# Thoughts and flowers

For every flower, there's a reason.
For every thought, there's a theme.
Let every flower find its season,
And every thought find its dream.

J.J.J.     John Allwork

# Theobalds Farm House

Down a seldom used old Crews Hill track,
Stands a house that dates some centuries back.
A large farm house now proudly shown,
Where a family here has made a home.

What of the families that have come and gone,
In Enfield's history their names live on.
Still fairly new on this Crews Hill scene,
Comes the garden designer Alison Green.

Her house is named in an Enfield entry,
And gives its date – mid seventeenth century.
Just who's passed through her garden gate,
A Prince or a Lord from a Royal estate?

And would this house perhaps confess,
Of seeing Dick Turpin on horse Black Bess!
Or even the Crews Hill, William Crews,
Had stayed for a night after too much booze!

We know Nigel Hawthorn, of acting fame,
Had walked quite often along this lane.
He'd seen a garden that looked forlorn,
Now bursting in bloom, with a spiral lawn!

The garden has a stream with a waterfall,
A woodland walk, and a swimming pool.
There's a trampoline for the fit and keen,
And a hot-tub near to keep you clean.

The garden's grown with skill and care,
With different sections to inspire and share.
A delight for people passing through…
On tired old land, grows a garden new!

J.J.J.          John Allwork

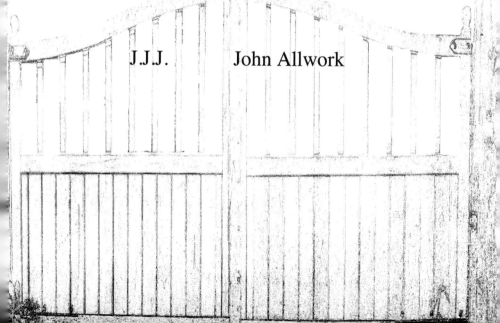

# The Ornamental Rock Dance

In the damp stillness of an evening,
Where moisture muffles sound.
The minute spot of a water drop,
Freezes as it hits the ground.

In the fading light of the evening,
With my daily gardening done,
I bid goodbye to the garden,
The garden, bids goodbye to the sun!

\* \* \*

Now long gone was the evening,
The black of night lay thick on the land.
A sudden shrill bark, from a fox in the dark,
Stirs statues from a daytime stand!

From all around the old garden,
Figures move from their personal posts.
From hedgerows and dark covered corners,
Come the stone cold outlines of ghosts!

Garden statues in a steady procession,
Break out of their statuesque stance.
They gather in the depths of the darkness,
For a nightly, Ornamental Rock Dance!

The rock Rabbit rumbas up to the Lion,
A Greek God grabs a Venus alone.
They waltz on the grass of the garden,
These classic lithe statues of stone!

The stone Duck sambas up to the Hedgehog,
The Mermaid simply wiggles her tail.
Now the party's begun, just one hour of fun,
As the squirrel pirouettes round a snail!

Frozen water flows from a fountain,
In these scenes too strange to believe.
Cold bonfires relight in the dead of the night,
A stone Adam kisses his Eve!

The heavy black breath of the night sky,
Filters through the twigs of the trees.
There's only one chance for the statues to dance,
Within the hour each figure then leaves!

They return to their plinths in the garden,
And resume their usual repose.
But, no one's aware of their night life...
(It's just the gardener, who secretly knows!)

J.J.J.    John Allwork

# Talking to Potatoes

Some people don't have to graft,
Some people don't have to toil,
Some people, escape physical work,
By using a verbal foil.

That's ok!

But, no matter how much you say,
No matter how clever you sound,
You just can't TALK a potato,
OUT of the ground!

Someone has to graft,
Someone has to toil,
Someone has to DIG,
The potato from the soil!

So, having looked at life,
Here's a fact I've found,
There's ALWAYS someone ready to…
TALK A POTATO OUT THE GROUND!

J.J.J.    John Allwork

# Lycopersicum esculentum

When the Boffins made up
The Latin plant names,
Their imaginations gathered momentum.
For why should the simple tomato
become . . .
Lycopersicum esculentum  !


J.J.J.      John Allwork

# Staying put

I could have gone to Blackpool,
I could have gone to Rome,
I could have gone to Brighton
But, I just wanted to stay at
home.


J.J.J.     John Allwork

# Change of mind

I'm sitting,   in a single seat,

With a sack,   I've packed before.

Left a note,  to say,  I won't be back,

Nor,  knock upon your door !

Hello !

J.J.J.      John Allwork

# Environmental Change

## No one left on the island

There's no one left on the island,
There's no one left to cry.
For the wave that came removed their name,
It was the wave that said,  goodbye


The Tsunami, a natural disaster,
Brought the environment into the home.
It tore through house bricks and the plaster,
And left thousands to wander alone.

Can we cope with all the great changes,
That Man has already made
To an Earth, controlled by high wages,
Where countries of wealth hold the stage!

With World sea levels rising,
As the ice melts at the Poles.
Our Planet, not really surprising,
Is struggling with climate controls.

The air is full of foul gases,
From our planes, lorries and vans.
It's poisoning us humans in masses . . .
But, (it's fox hunting the government bans!)

Will governments help our old Planet?
The environment is in need of a hand.
Or, will it be a "green", John and Janet,
Who make the FINAL last stand?


There's no one left on our island,
Our island has been, washed away.
For the waves that roll, have taken their toll.
(Scientists said, this would happen one day)


J.J.J.    John Allwork

# Eleventh September 2001

Those hankies waved in despair
Fell with bodies in mid-air.
And perished beneath this man made state…
The crushing weight of human hate!

Will a God somewhere now draw the line
Between men of good and men of crime,
For mortal man must bow his head…
He's seen the living become the dead!

J.J.J.　　John Allwork

# Final Words

## From Two Wounded Soldiers

1:        "I think of you, your brown eyes blazing!"

2:        "I picture you, your blue eyes bright!"

1 & 2:   "We think of home and life's amazing!"

But no one heard their words that night.

...Two more casualties of war.

J.J.J.    John Allwork

*( a ribbon of glass has to be measured every five minutes*
*to a depth of two inches )*

## Ged's Glass Factory

I'm sitting, watching, waiting, watching,
This moving tongue of moving glass.
I'm sitting, watching, clocking, the minutes as they pass.
No one flinches,
Two inches, two inches.

Along comes Bill, brother of Bert,
Same shirt, same dirt.
By the boiler sits the oiler, squeaking out a joke,
Same bloke, same joke.
He heaves himself up, and tends to the winches,
Looks at John, five minutes have gone,
And, two inches, two inches.

I hear our Phyl, sister of Jill,
Same blouse, same rows.
Near the furnace fiery Ernest, chills out with a mate,
Same mate , same fate.
They pull up a chain, a vessel it lynches.
I bide my time, five minutes are mine,
Then, two inches, two inches.

I see the cleaner, a dusty dreamer,
Sweeping floors of stone.
Cleaning for the Factory, dreaming of her Home.
Clean on, dream on.
I loosen my belt it pinches,
Then look for a sign, five minutes of time,
And, two inches, two inches.

I'm sitting, clocking, counting the cracks upon the wall.
I'm sitting, clocking, counting the minutes as they fall.
The time ticks away, in twelve's every hour,
No sign of nature, neither a bird nor flower,
No roses or robins, no sparrows or finches,
But, in five minutes time . . .
Two inches, two inches.


J.J.J.    John Allwork

The Unsung Hero

He never gets into the papers,
He never gets into the news.
He works all day earns his way,
And pays his daily dues.

He's always crushed in the rush hour
And always soaked in the rain.
Always first in the work place,
And always the last to remain.

He never asks for more money,
Though his fares increase on the train.
He goes unseen in the work place,
Because He's the LAST to complain.

He never takes time off for sickness,
He battles it out with the flu.
He has only one weakness,
He is just SO honestly true !

He's friendly to people who greet him,
And the best friend I've ever had.
I'd hoped one day you could meet him,
This hero, unsung was my Dad !

J.J.J.   John Allwork

# The Prattaperu

When things go wrong, he's someone to blame,
Stupid things done became known by his name.
Why accidents happened he hadn't a clue,
But they were all linked to the PRATTAPERU !

You're walking quite straight then suddenly wobble
On pavements so flat, you go home with a hobble !
Why this should happen isn't blamed upon you,
It's due to the approaching . . . PRATTAPERU !

You wash white shirts with a jumper that's new,
Whitest of whites, change to a delicate blue !
A mistake was made, this much is true . . .
But the blame is laid upon the PRATTAPERU !

In the middle of cooking you take a short break,
Your soft sponge pudding dries to a flake !
The fault's not yours, nor your recipe new,
For the cook in control is the PRATTAPERU !

You're part of the party, part of the fun . . .
Queuing for hours to see a film's first run.
You study your tickets, you've been in the wrong queue !
It's then you concur, you're the PRATTAPERU !

You fill car with petrol, and head off for home,
Then realise the car, is a diesel you own !
You chug to a halt, now what do you do ?
You're the driver in charge and the PRATTAPERU !

You check name of theatre, and arrive on time,
But instead of your Opera, you listen to Mime !
You've not checked dates the Opera was due . . .
With seated spectators hides the PRATTAPERU !

When people quite normal, for one moment given,
Do something stupid . . . they should be forgiven.
So PLEASE don't mention, or give us a clue,
If someone you knew was, the PRATTAPERU !

J.J.J.    John Allwork

A view across the Exe near Lympstone.

# THE WEEKEND!

## THE LONDON RUSH TO DEVON GOES

## AND I RACE TO TOPSHAM TOWN...!

With  timeless  tides  a  river  flows,

And      the      pace      of      life

Slows      down.

J.J.J.      John Allwork

The Goat Walk looking towards
Topsham.

# The Goat Walk

In the tidal town of Topsham,
Resting in Devon by the sea,
Lies a low curving walkway
Where I often wish to be  !

With its wall and narrow pathway,
It leans its back against the land,
Its stone legs against the sea,
And stone feet upon the sand.

You can still sense people passing,
Though they've long since passed away
From this little ledge of concrete,
Where their dreams still rest today!

Bathing beautifully in the sunshine,
Bare and bleak in winter gales.
It sits with seats of people's names ,
Where once they told their tales.

Relax a while on the Goat Walk,
And  enjoy  the  estuary  air.
Delight in the view, seen by the few
Who leave their names on a chair !


J.J.J.    John Allwork

# The Exe at Topsham

An open river, an open mind
An open landscape, with sky behind.
A distant shore across the Exe,
An ancient history of ships and wrecks.

A Vast expanse of sea and sky,
That, mirrored image as life drifts by.
Such was the river that I sailed on,
A new bridge built, some old boys gone!

A Western train by this western river,
With a human cargo to deliver.
Those children full of holiday fun
See the sparkling Exe on its sea bound run.

Wild waters swirl, an endless weave,
Those hidden mud flats do deceive.
While swans with cygnets enjoy a swim,
The country church sings a Christian hymn.

Upon this river my dreams will float,
And voyage one day on an unseen boat.
Returning , with every summer's sun,
To where the sea, and sky, and I, are one.


J.J.J.    John Allwork

# The Tonic of Topsham

Tension down, unwind that frown,
Take in the tonic that's Topsham Town.

Walk to the river with reed beds wide,
And watch the sunlit sea birds glide.
Their flashing flocks form a constant roll,
Following fish in a fleeing shoal.

Thousands feeding at low tide,
Bird beaks moving side to side.
A place where man has space to share,
Where birds and sail boats use the air.

So forget the strain of city strife,
Leave long behind that London life.
Come stroll along a Topsham street,
Where friendly shops and shoppers meet.

To the Goat Walk, where the river bends,
And Old Topsham Town, gently ends.


J.J.J.    John Allwork

# In a Topsham Tavern.

Such a perfect place to begin,
Lunchtime, in the Lighter Inn!
With a sandwich fresh and hot meal too,
And a welcome pint of Badger's Brew.

Supping a beer on a sunny seat,
With a quayside view, quite a treat!
Watching the yachts go sailing past,
Wishing this time would last and last!

This Topsham Tavern I had once known,
Now miles away from my London home!

J.J.J.    John Allwork

# To
## Kirsty in the Sunshine

I couldn't help but remember you
Sunbathing there that day.
The sun was hot, the weather warm
And, you were lying in my way.

I spaced my steps politely,
To avoid your female form
Relaxing in the sunshine
On, an Exeter City lawn.

I left, Kirsty in the sunshine,
And my brother Bill upon his boat.
A vessel quite intriguing
On which Kirsty wrote a nautical note.

We thank you for your story
In, The Devon Life magazine,
Which highlighted the history
Of, Bill's boat and lifeboat scene.

I dream of a sunny Exeter
With seagulls on masts so tall,
The sunbathers and harbour folk,
Listen long to the seagulls call.

*

The seagulls call to wish you well,
We all join in along the quay.
Best wishes from "Charles Dibdin"
Its Captain Bill, and me!


J.J.J.   John Allwork

111

Bill's boats 'Charles Dibdin and
Charlie', centre picture, with the
new flats behind.

# The Albatross of Exeter

Now I ain't much with words,
'Cos there's better blokes than me,
Who can put words together
And tell a true story of the sea.

I journey down from London,
And in your Exeter I stay.
But, each visit to your marina
I see more boats have gone away!

They keep on building houses,
New flats now swamp the boats!
What happened to those vessels
And all those maritime blokes?

Wandering curves of the Quayside
Spread like the wings of a bird.
I'll call it, The "Albatross" of Exeter,
And under threat, so I've heard!

Now, I ain't much with words,
But I do know what I see...
People in a powerful place,
Removing Exeter from the sea!

They'll fill in the marina,
Then empty the old canal,
And fill it with a road
It's much more cheap somehow!

Now, I ain't much with words,
And some ain't much with boats
And some ain't much on history,
Of all those maritime blokes.

Will Exeter kill its "ALBATROSS,"
The most symbolic of our birds,
By removing sailors and their Port...
But then,
I ain't much with words!


J.J.J.    John Allwork

# Rabbits of the Seas.

The harbour is home to houses,
Where a marina moored its boats.
The marina moves to another site
Where, NOTHING in it floats!

There is a new proposal,
To move the marina site.
To a dry green playing field
Where rabbits graze at night!

It is hard for an outsider
To try and understand,
Why build houses in a harbour
And a marina on dry land?

Just who planned this move
For the future of the boats,
To be stored in a dry field
Where rabbits eat their oats!

Dry boats in a dry marina,
In a field fenced with trees,
Penned like orphaned animals,
Trapped, "Rabbits of the Seas!"

Why can't boats in a marina
Have clear access to the sea?
Via a liquid knows as water,
On which boats ARE meant to be!

This move saves council money,
And the treasurer it'll please!
But, don't let your boats become...
The "RABBITS OF THE SEAS!"


J.J.J.   John Allwork

A view of the Exeter Basin.

# EXETER

## A Quay Issue!

I once met a man of Exeter
A boat building on the quay.
Both man and a maritime legend
Living history you could see...!

Our proud old port of Exeter
With boats maintained with pride.
Now struggles for its history,
Which is ebbing with the tide.

Four hundred years boat business
Centre solidly on the quay.
How long will the quay continue
Supporting, vessels for the sea?

The City's greatest asset,
It's quays fed a nautical trade.
But, boats which brought the riches in
Now seem mostly doomed to fade!

They might replace our boatyards,
AND move boats maintained with pride.
But CAN they replace a history
Which flows in on every tide?

Who said in Exeter City :-
"The boats have served their time?"
Will houses stand where boats once stood
On OUR HISTORY-------MARITIME!

What of this blow to history,
Will it turn the tourist trade
Away from a famous waterfront,
Will commercial ventures fade?

New buildings on the quayside
Remove boats maintained with pride.
But, they can't remove our history
For it flows in on every tide!

So where's the Man of Exeter
A boat building on the Quay?
Both Man and a maritime legend,
ARE NO LONGER THERE TO SEE!


J.J.J.    John Allwork

# The Lympstone Lady

## To Sarah

The Lympstone Lady is tall and slim,
The Lympstone Lady simply,
waits for him.
The Lympstone Lady with eyes
blue and bright,
Watches his boat sail through the night!

J.J.J.      John Allwork

# The old railway arch near Tiverton
## (Anni's Arch)

The tunnel is Tiverton  history,
Its arch, a span of time.
I cycled there one summer
With, a very good friend of mine.

\* \* \* \*

All that's left is a silent arch,
Smoky trains have ceased their march.

An empty tunnel, this forgotten scene,
Those shiny tracks return to green.

The tunnel breathes the tranquil air,
A thoughtful stillness lingers there.

Wild flowers grow where trains had been,
On this line that saw the end of steam.

Gone are the passengers, gone are the crew,
The arch remains where lives passed through.

\* \* \* \*

I cycled there one summer,
Upon this arch I spent some time.
On the tunnel of Tiverton history
I stood . . . with a friend of mine.


J.J.J.    John Allwork

121

# The unwritten postcard

I bought you a postcard,
I haven't sent.
Tried to write the words,
I truly meant.
I will send the card,
Perhaps one day.
When I find the words,
I wish to say!


J.J.J.    John Allwork

York.

The Hole in the Wall, Pub.

To Myra.


The close comfort of a cosy Inn,
Where familiar strangers soon walk in.
Such as we found on our trip to York,
A peaceful place to eat…
And time to talk.


J.J.J.          John Allwork

## Part of a Cargo

The ticketed traveller,
On a clickerty train,
The Newspaper unraveller
Off to work again.

He's suited and routed
For the old City Centre,
He's crushed and rushed
Through a week long adventure.

He travels with people,
Knows not their names,
He's part of a cargo,
Carried by trains!


J.J.J.    John Allwork

A tribute to my mother and the bowling group she started in Enfield for people with Parkinson's.

## Taking Part In Bowls

Five circles, the Olympic Games,
Mega Bucks – with famous names!
Cheered by crowds to the winning line,
A medal won for the winning time!

From the Olympic symbol,
To us bowlers, less nimble.
We draw a much smaller crowd,
And play our games, no famous names,
But end up, feeling so PROUD!

We have our circles around our eyes,
And a heavy handicap, to overcome!
But,
     We have no need for a winning line,
For,
     In taking part
               we know
                    WE'VE WON!

J.J.J.    John Allwork

# A Question of Sport

The Major and I and a handful of men,
Stand ready for battle, at the head of the Glen.
Our fire-arms loaded we study the sky,
Awaiting our quarry – ready to die.

Game birds our quest, both cock and hen,
We're but a handful, against a thousand of them.
To most outsiders, we might look absurd,
In uniform we're clothed, to mimic a bird.

Our foe are feathered, down to the knees,
We dress likewise, short trousers deceive.
Lower leg protection, against weather and rock,
Covered by tradition, with a good sturdy sock.

Even our hats they come to peak,
Built to resemble a formidable beak.
To the birds, these clothes appear not to shock,
They're cleverly contrived, so we look like a flock.

Thus quite exposed, the harsh weather we feel,
Our only comforts are our shotguns of steel.
With nothing of interest, few things to do,
We gaze for a while, and take in the view.

Up from the ground, like sudden dust storms,
Come clouds upon clouds of feathery forms.
Battle is waged against this gruesome game,
The numbers killed will bring us all fame.

A few ounces of feathers, against pounds of lead,
Birds fall from the sky, heavily dead.
Brave are the lads their faces so stern,
They hold the line standing straight and firm.

A victorious day, we head happily for home,
While on the moor, blood drips from a stone:
A flowing red epitaph to this sport of men
Colours crimson the ground of this Glorious Glen.

The old Major and I and many men,
Wait again for the birds, just a handful of them.
Once so numerous in this famous Glen,
We're faced with the question, what "sport" is it THEN?


J.J.J.    John Allwork

# Sam the dog

Sam the dog is known to bark,
From early morn to after dark.
He guards his place of that, no doubt,
Lets no one in, and no one out.

Sam rushes out his house to chase
Any member of the human race;
Any bird or beast, cloud or fly,
Anything, innocently passing by.

Even motorbike boys with helmets on,
He'd eat the weak he'd eat the strong.
There was something about THIS head-ware,
So, to passing bikers – "DO BEWARE!"

Of other dogs he comes to meet,
They keep THEIR distance at forty feet.
But Sam had friends – it's true to say,
He digs them up in a playful way.

Sam waters plants – not just in drought,
And the neighbour's Lupines weren't left out.
For he was caught in the midst of duty,
And called indoors for defacing beauty.

His Master's voice rang out so clear –
"SAM! YOU BLOODY DOG COME HERE!"


J.J.J.    John Allwork

## Goodbye to Kai

That wagging tail would never fail,
To greet her master home each day.
With a gleeful eye the gamesome Kai,
Would welcome any chance of play.

This football freak, had a habit unique,
And rarely passed her ball to her chums.
She'd chew the ball all day and all week,
Until her teeth wore down to her gums!

Through her family home, Kai loved to roam,
And into the garden she'd willingly race.
Her parting now we all bemoan . . .
We've lost a much loved family face!

No more the ride by her master's side,
Those van rides have come to an end.
"The Orchards," her home she'd guard with pride,
And where rests, our four footed friend!

J.J.J.   John Allwork

# Efficiency or Indifference

(Theft reported to Police at 17:00 hours,
June 29<sup>th</sup> 2011)

I filled in a Police theft form,

On June Twenty Nine.

Of my van contents stolen,

I reported the crime!

I received a Police letter,

Dated, June Twenty Nine.

Saying, They've closed the case,

On the report of this crime!

That was quick!

J.J.J.     John Allwork

# Children's Section

Some members of the crew on board
the Charles Dibdin.

# Christmas in the Cosmos

With Christmas round the corner,
We have Orion in the sky
And winter winds to chill us,
As we burn the Guy Fawkes' guy.

While, up above the clouds,
Beyond our planet Earth,
Stars see historic scenes
Like the famous Christmas birth.

Planet Venus was a witness,
Shining with the stars.
It twinkles nearest the Earth
Between Mercury and Mars.

Our thoughts return to Christmas,
And the annual festive fun,
As the Earth and all the planets
Slowly circle around the Sun.

Such a circle of importance,
Giving Earth both night and day . . .
So that Santa can come to my Town
I hope it's HERE he parks his sleigh !

J.J.J.    John Allwork

# Gnat not Nat
## A plea for my G

I'm a small gnat, not a great gnu.
My 'G' is silent and a good job too.
I'd hate to be a Ger-nat,
It would bring too much fame!
There'd be poems about me,
Just to sound off my name.
I'll go quietly through life,
With my silent 'G'.
But, don't forget to include it,
When you write about me!


J.J.J.     John Allwork

# On Being Official
## (Or as Harry thought, a-fish-shoal)

Harry had herrings hanging from his head
Such a strange sight,
I thought something should be said…
"Harry, why do you have herrings,
Hanging from your head?"
Harry said,
"I was told to be a-fish-shoal,
I've an important day ahead!"


J.J.J.　　John Allwork

# The House Fairies.

Of fairies in the garden, you'd find three or four,
Venture inside, and you'd find several more.

For who left the butter out all night,
Who squeezed the toothpaste with all their might.

Why was there jam on the kitchen floor,
When it had been perfectly clean the night before.

That piece of puzzle no one had found,
Suddenly seen by the clock when that was wound.

The missing shoe from under my bed,
Turned up with the key to the garden shed.

And how did the toy, that was lost all day,
Re-appear in the morning ready to play.

Such strange events that go on in the night,
But basically house fairies put most things right.


J.J.J.    John Allwork

## Why is it?

Why is it, wasps have wings,
And attack us quickly with their stings?
While the humble bumblebee is kind,
And makes its honey for us to find!

Why is it, when mosquitoes bite,
They seem to do so over night?
While the naughty gnat has no night time play,
But will happily bite throughout the day!

Why is it, when bath time draws near,
Big bathroom spiders reappear?
While the silverfish to our delight,
Disappear quickly out of sight!

Why is it, when it's time for bed,
I've a million things that should be said?
But in the morning when it's time to rise,
I find it hard, just to open my eyes!

Why is it, when things go wrong,
They seem to do so, for so long?
Then magically some hand of might,
Mostly puts the wrongs to right!


J.J.J.    John Allwork

137

# Never , see me praying

I couldn't be bothered at Lunchtime

I couldn't be bothered at Tea,

I couldn't be bothered to thankyou,

For all the food you've brought to me.


You'll  NEVER  see me praying,

NEVER  see me bow me head.

( But secretly I thankyou Lord,

When I'm tucked up in me bed ! )


J.J.J.    John Allwork

## On Being,
## A twelve year old female.


We just can't get up in the morning,
We simply must go to bed late at night.
We are now in our twelve's
We should think for ourselves,
And, we're sure at this age this is right!

We simply can't choose clothes with our Parents,
For dress-sense they haven't at all.
They put things on wrong
Choose a fashion that's gone,
And colours that would simply appal.

We simply can't eat out with our Parents,
They embarrass us right from the start.
They choose a plain venue
We get an under twelve's' menu,
While THEY chose a choice á la carte.

We simply can't go to museums with our Parents,
We just don't like museums at all.
They teach us about facts
Of historic names upon plaques,
WELL, we might as well be back at school.

We simply can't watch T.V. with our Parents,
Their choice of programmes drive us quite MAD!
All they like is the News
Or some literary muse,
And they think the SOAPS are all bad.

BUT, we simply can't have Christmas without Parents,
Now at Christmas we'll excuse their odd fault.
For, the thought that brings joy
To us females so coy,
Is, of those presents we hope they have bought!


J.J.J.    John Allwork

# Higgidy Pie

I spy a Higgidy Pie,
Hidding in the bag of a passer by.

This triggered off a train of thought,
Now THAT'S the pie I wished I'd bought!

J.J.J.    John Allwork

# Kimble the Cat!

Kimble the Cat, ate fish by himself,
Though he wasn't a selfish Cat.
For he'd miaow for his tea
He'd do tricks for free,
But singing, no one dared to ask THAT!

In singing a story he'd sing very poorly,
With notes going right off the scale.
While Kimble stayed calm
Cats showed their alarm,
With a flick and a swish of the tail.

He'd tell tall tales of Fishes and Whales,
Thus telling a whale of a tale.
But the problem in truth-
And his voice was the proof . . .
His tale was just wail after wail.

Now Kimble the Cat, he thought about that,
His own noise he couldn't abide.
A music teacher he'd ring
To teach him to sing,
Then he could tell his tales with some pride!


Cats though they ought, have never been taught,
To sing to a melodious scale.
Now it's Kimble who's King
And people pay him to sing . . .
About, the loss of the wail in his tale !


J.J.J.    John Allwork

143

# The Mickleton Moggie

The Mickleton moggie the size of a doggie,
Prowled along lanes late at night.
Such was the fear, no one went near
This moggie with a HUGE appetite.

Only last week in the middle of sleep,
Poor Richard ( the third ) he digested,
And the Merchant of Venice whilst playing his tennis,
Went just the same way, it's suggested !

Of Henry ( the fifth) there still hangs the myth
About the moggie in the hamlet that day.
Henry disappeared into the moggie it's feared,
In a comedy of errors, so they say !

When he fancies a snack he's quick to attack,
And rarely is the cat to be beaten.
He'd hold his foe, and then say very low . . .
" To be, or not to be…eaten ?"

Two gentlemen of Verona whose general persona
Fitted measure for measure a dark crime.
They looked very pale in this winter's tale,
But I'll tell THAT story next time !

The Mickleton moggie with weather quite foggy,
On the twelfth night after the tempest.
Had trouble galore with a tooth in his jaw,
And slunk off to find a good dentist.

He came to a scene a midsummer nights dream,
With an Ass called Bottom that frowned,
A musician conducted, the director instructed
That actors , please sit on the ground.

Out shot a shrill , whistle like trill,
From the Ass that sat on a thistle.
The director then wrote this historical note,
" I've heard the first Bottom to whistle !"

Off shot the cat he didn't like that,
For the whistle was part of a spell.
He's now taming a shrew and is good,
through and through.
Hence, all's well that ends well !

J.J.J.    John Allwork

# Don't get stuck this Christmas

The Mickleton moggie on Michaelmas day,
Saw Santa fly by, on a magical sleigh.
He called up to Santa, " I've a parcel for you,
Please deliver directly to 4 Norton View!"

Santa flew down and picked up the parcel,
Headed for Mickleton, to a princess in her castle.
Passing Inns and Hotels that welcome a guest
He stopped at the Pudding Club, (just for a rest) ...

Though Santa's arrival took guests by surprise,
The sight before Santa was a feast for his eyes,
He saw steaming great puddings, ready to eat . . .
And was invited to stay, for a Michaelmas treat.

Santa ate seven puddings and picked out the best,
Then found that his tummy felt tight with his vest.
Old Santa stood up, to return to his sledge,
But stuck in the doorway just like a wedge.

Our moggie soon heard of Santa's great plight,
And feared of his parcel, not arriving that night.
He raced to the Pudding Club, saw Santa's red coat
Sticking out of the doorway like the bow of a boat!

He asked for permission to drive the great sleigh
In a last minute effort to get his parcel away.
He held the sleigh reins with muddy great paws,
Became Mickleton's hero, and was called
"Santa Claws"

Well I do know this story has many flaws.
But the Pudding Club now, has widened its doors,
And Michaelmas day, the 29th of September
Is a day that Santa is advised to remember.


Don't get stuck this Christmas!


J.J.J.    John Allwork

Ludovic Von
Strudel Scoffen

# Ludovic Von Strudel Scoffen

Many a food parcel left Scrumpschloss castle,
Travelling across its Battenburg Bridge,
So named by the baker our master cake maker,
Who designed each pie with a ridge.

Ludovic Von Strudel Scoffen,
Cooked in his kitchen offen,
And made oodles of strudels and pies.
He looked very grand with cook book in hand
And flour dust outlining his eyes.

He had a pet poodle
That was partial to strudel,
And would bark should a cake thief appear.
It would crouch on all fours and guard oven doors
If a stranger wandered too near.

They would dress very dapper
Chef and pet "woofen schnapper"…
( It's Austrian for dog, don't you know! )
One of their thrills was a walk in the hills
And return to the oven's warm glow.

Now, a cockerel would sing,
To an oven clock's ring,
Telling Ludovic his pies were cooked through.
It didn't sing the most conventional thing
But, would crow, "Cock-a-strudel-do!"

One day while out walking,
Along with barking and stalking,
The poodle found an Austrian hat
This gave chef an idea that soon became clear,
He'd design a cake based on that!

So the Hat Cake took form
And a new expression was born
Which came to sum up a selling success.
He made no mistakes for, "Selling like Hat Cakes!"
Became the phrase Ludovic loved to express!

When next you go shopping
And your thoughts turn to scoffing
Some scrumptious pastry or pie.
For Ludovic's sake, ask for a Hat Cake,
It would please him, if you bought one to try!


J.J.J.    John Allwork


150

## Ludovic von two
## The battle of Scrumpschloss Castle

The hills were alive with the smell of baking,
Everyone knew it was of Ludovic's making.
The Germans sent out their dessert spies,
To question the Austrian with flour round his eyes.

Their quest to discover the hat cake's success,
And a talk with Ludovic to make him confess.
The hat cake recipe was an Austrian secret,
Of such importance the Nation needed to keep it !

So help was required within the Chef's house,
Friends came along and among them was Klaus.
Klaus von Coffen Offen, was Ludovic's cousin,
A poorly old boy who caught colds by the dozen !

Klaus checked door locks and secured the keys,
He tried not to cough, and stifled a sneeze.
He'd brought along his special old hen,
A talking bird that could mimic men.

Such a rare bird, no one thought it was real,
For this talking hen was a, Cluckenspiel !
Another female to help, and an Austrian winner,
Was cake throwing champion, Frau Flan Flinger !

Ludovic's idea was but, "pie in the sky,"
"Never mind that" coughed Klaus, "give it a try!"
"Frau Flinger could throw weighty fresh pies"
"To be aimed directly at the incoming spies!"

With Cluckenspiel ready, and Frau Flinger in place,
Ludovic's security had stepped up a pace.
From the castle's top tower, the hen could see danger,
With keen eyesight could soon spy a stranger.

The hen informed Frau "dessert spies are about!"
Flinger flung a pie, and knocked a spy out !
Spy seeking cakes were cooked in the castle,
They had a candle on top to light up the rascal !

So pie after pie soon found its mark,
And illuminous pastry was used after dark !
A glowing red cake landed square on a spy,
It had a candle on top which lit up the sky !

Town folk came round and soon formed a ring,
Around this candle lit spy, who then started to sing . . .
"It's my Birthday today, and I wish now to say,
Just why did I spy, it's my Birthday today !"

The crowd made a wish, and blew his candle out.
For he'd learnt his lesson, of that no doubt.
The Cluckenspiel clucked, "It's time to clock off"
Klaus agreed, as he'd started to cough !

Frau Flinger called out, "Just one more throw!"
The spies had enough, it was high time to go.
The spies headed home with a blank recipe,
While Ludovic and friends had hat cakes for tea !

From this day on, candles are placed on a cake,
As a birthday treat, with a wish you can make.
Your friends close by – Happy Birthday they'll sing,
As you blow out the candles of a flame lit ring !


J.J.J.    John Allwork

# My Shadow

I saw my shadow
Upon the wall,

And I thought

That's all!

J.J.J.            John Allwork

# P.G. and the Horse Race

Our character's name and hero no doubt,
Was known for his drinking of Tea.
And called throughout as Percival Grout,
Though shortened by friends to P.G.

Now, P.G. owned a Scottish horse,
With the curious name of Stilton.
More curious still it could neigh in morse,
And always had a kilt on.

Its family, "Mc Dougal."
Joined many a cavalry charge.
They could also play the bugle,
Which certainly pleased the Serg.

They'd go out to ride in the countryside,
People who saw them laughed.
Tartan dress on horse hide,
But it covered up the draught!

P.G's town of Odourado,
Famed for its abundance of cheese.
Was a stopping place for Wells Fargo,
But not if there wasn't a breeze.

The town held an annual horse race,
During the month of June.
Starting at the market-place,
Where the band played a tune.

The horses were to begin on the flat,
This being shown on the tellies.
But not to cross the watery tract,
Owing to the lack of wellies.

Across the river by some fords,
Lived a lively looking fella.
The Blacksmith who mended swords,
And was a general metal seller.

Competitors for the race-

The Doctor ventured one of his nags,
A healthy looking filly.
He registered her as Tea Bags,
And would run if it wasn't too chilly.

The Vicar's horse, a timid mare,
Daily ate the sweetest hay.
Nightly she said a prayer,
To keep her rivals away.

The blacksmith registered his horse,
And 'Anvil' was its name.
Not known for speed, only force,
Such power had brought him fame.

Standing riveted with pride,
This hefty, bulky, beast,
Of seven feet high, four feet wide,
And weighing a ton at least.

On the eve of the horse race…

One could find P.G. in the officials hut,
As it was his turn to do the betting.
The door left open never shut,
For he'd cheat if anyone let him.

The journalists, with pens in hand,
Were there to write a story.
They listened to the village band,
Waiting for something more gory.

The sports writer – so very polite,
Went into the officials shed.
And asked P.G. the horse he liked,
His reply- The Doctor's, she's ahead.

Thus ran the headlines in the local Mags:-
"P.G. tips Tea Bags!"

J.J.J.    John Allwork

The horse race continued...

## Trouble at the race track.

Such were the events as they stood,
Not quite as they might appear.
Some people were up to no good,
A talking point for the rest of the year!

The troublesome men, the worst of the bunch,
Could be found at the end of the bar.
They knocked back beer and crunched their lunch
And spat bones out, ever so far.

They were Dynamite Damper and Picnic Hamper,
And were known to the local law.
No one should tackle or tamper
With these villains, who'd been arrested before.

Now Dynamite played with gun powder,
Being explosive like his name.
While Picnic was fond of cooking,
Being troublesome all the same.

They catered in explosive foods,
Well known out in the West.
Suited most tastes and different moods,
Their beans and bangers being the best.

Back to the actual horse race,
Where the day was bright and sunny.
The officials worked at a frantic pace,
While a Frenchman counted his money.

He was Blaireau Bill, Ze French fur trader.
Who went into the saloon,
Had a drink with June,
And left, but never paid her!

Dynamite Damper and Picnic Hamper,
Planed to pillage Bill's fur pelts.
But they were tied on to his horse
By a number of strong leather belts.

Dynamite deftly set his trap,
To explode in front of Bill's horse.
This to happen on the very last lap,
With sticks of dynamite providing the force!

Blaireau Bill had a name for his nag,
He called her Silver Lining.
She was bought in gold from an old hag,
In the mountains where he'd been mining.

With horses under starters orders,
And P.G. closing the betting,
The crowd crushed to the racetrack borders,
As Dynamite chose the right setting.

They're off!

The pace was set by the Doctor's horse,
With hooves making a thunderous roar.
They galloped along over granite and gorse,
Not knowing what was in store.

Dynamite was so thirsty,
He knocked back some stout.
Picnic had some winkles,
He tried to wiggle one out.

The last lap, well under way,
Silver Lining was lagging behind.
She'd wanted to win the race all day...
Summoned all the strength she could find.

Tea Bags, placing her faith in the Gods,
Careered round the course so fast.
Was well aware, that some sort of clods
Had passed her, with a blast.

For Dynamite set off the explosion,
In order to get to the furs...
But, the first things past the finishing post,
Were a saddle and a pair of spurs.

Silver Lining raced up to the sky,
Wearing clouds of furs around her.
She looked well dressed, just lacked a tie,
And that's how the Good Lord found her.

Some whites and silvers from her furs,
Settled in the clouds, so high.
Now locals reflect when memory stirs,
How clouds became so colourful, and why.

Most pelts rained down at a gentle pace;
Silver is happy in Heaven, not whining.
For HER saddle and spurs had won the race,
Hence, every cloud has a silver lining...


J.J.J.    John Allwork

# Back to boats

Bill's boat, 'Charles Dibdin' in Paluden.

# Paluden

The peaceful Port of Paluden,
Should be witnessed at first hand,
To see the embrace of Mother Nature,
As the sea kisses the land.

Sailors worn out by a voyage
On boats battered by the sea.
Slip thankfully into this Port
Of, old French tranquillity.

There's no buzz of modern life
Nor, no Café upon the quay.
No tourist trade, no fortunes made
Just, pure nature, boats and me.

For here you hear the Earth breathe
On every still and sunlit day,
And where the torment of the sea,
Is soon gently soothed away.

Steep hills of sweet chestnut trees
Protect and watch the river glide.
Bird songs abound, a landscape of sound
As the river fills with every tide.

There's a house or two, with a river view
With French friends who show they care.
There's peace anew for an exhausted crew,
And there's a slipway for all to share.

In years to come, when my sailing's done.
I know my life will nothing lack.
For, I've sailed with my Brother Bill
To PALUDEN and back!


J.J.J.   John Allwork

# Friendships

Ships may come,

and Ships may go,

As they sail through stormy weather.

So Friends may come,

and Friends may go.

But, Friendships will last for ever !

J.J.J.     John Allwork